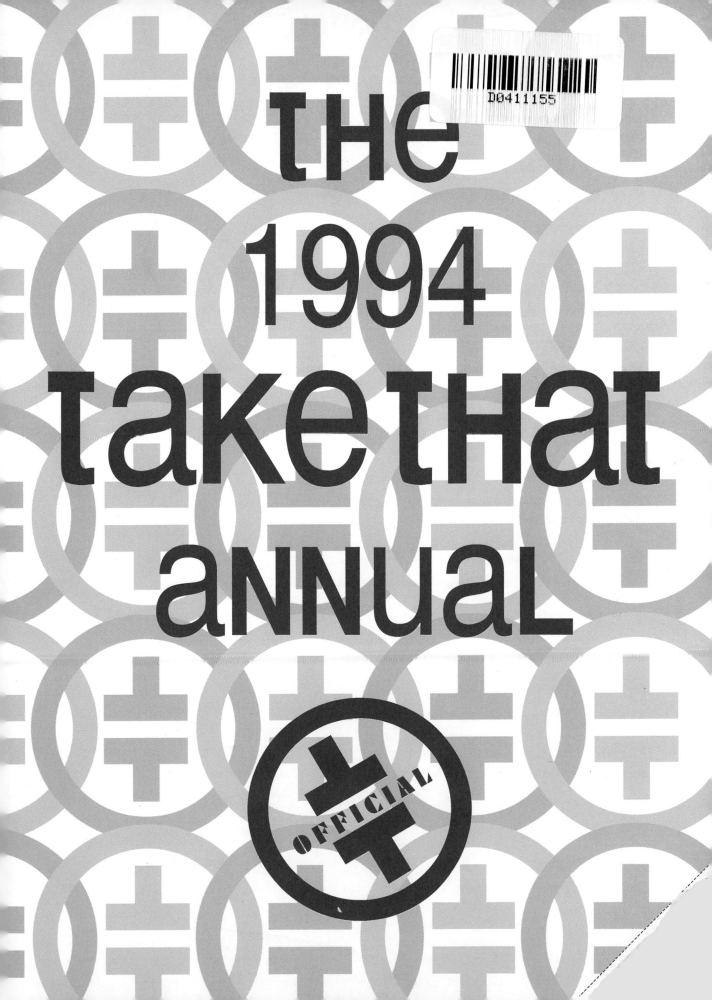

THE 1994 TAKE THAT ANNUAL

OFFICIAL

CONTENTS

⊕ take that

Hello
Welcome to our first annual

We're all really excited about it and we hope
you enjoy reading it as much as we enjoyed
putting it together. Our friend Alex from 'Smash Hits'
helped us out with writing it and she's a dead smart
journalist so everything you read is very accurate.
Read on and enjoy... Love Jason xo

Take Thats own annual, now ten years ago when I read
through my Beano, Elvis and Shoot (Football) annual I would never
have dreamt that one day I'd be in one, so excited and hopeful
on a Thursday afternoon we sit in our manager's, Nigel's, House
in Manchester with our mate Alex answering question after question,
some original, some not, trying to write a book that you, the
people that have made this happen, will enjoy. So as you turn
the page to read on, stay happy, stay safe and have a good day?
Love you Mark!
xo

Welcome to our first annual. We've had your support for the last three years and here we are having your support one more time. I'm sure you've heard us saying this many times before but we've all grateful and very proud of all you Take Thatters. keep up the interest we all love you very much. Stay safe and be careful.

Gaz

xxxxx

I hope by reading this annual you will discover a lot of things you never knew about us. I would also like you to realize, You are the reason that this annual has been made. Without you there wouldn't be a TAKE THAT. So THANKS

Howard x Donald x

HOPE THIS ANNUAL BRINGS SOME "TAKE THATNESS!" TO YOUR LIFE, CAN'T WRITE ANYMORE THAN THE OTHER LADS, SO I WON'T!

Love Robbie

the PERSONAL BITS

JASON

THE SCENE:
We do this interview in Nigel's big lounge. In the background, the rest of the lads are grouped round the television watching videos and later, the cricket, so there's much shouting and hollering at the telly. Jason is stretched out on the floor wearing a blue and white cotton shirt, blue cut down shorts, brown boots and black Adidas socks. He hasn't had a shave for a few days so he's looking a bit rugged (or scruffy, whichever you prefer!). He's eating one of the vegetarian salad sandwiches which Nigel has just brought over.

WHAT'S YOUR FULL NAME? *Jason Thomas Orange.*

HOW TALL ARE YOU? *Six foot.*

HOW MUCH DO YOU WEIGH? *11 stone 7lbs.*

WHERE DO YOU LIVE? *In Manchester with my brother, Simon.*

WHAT'S HAPPENING WITH THE HAIR? *I don't know. . . I like keeping it short because everyone else has theirs long and I like to be different! I chopped my Mohican out. I'm not having one any more. And I shaved my moustache off and most of the beard but I don't know where it's going. I bought some clippers and Gary's been cutting it recently. He's done a good job.*

WHAT'S YOUR INSIDE LEG MEASUREMENT? *34".*

SHOE SIZE? *Eight or eight and a half.*

DO YOU WEAR BOXER SHORTS OR BRIEFS? *Briefs. I just wear them because they're comfortable. I wear nice ones - they don't have to have a name attached to them, but I don't wear cheap rubbish. I just get them from any big department store, really, Marks and Spencer or wherever.*

WHAT DO YOU SPEND YOUR MONEY ON? *I tend to be quite generous with my friends and family and not generous enough with myself. I don't buy myself much although I have just bought myself some new clothes as a treat. But I like to save really.*

CAN YOU COOK? *Yeah. Not anything great, but I can make a good curry. I like curry.*

WHAT'S YOUR WORST HOUSEHOLD CHORE? *Cleaning the windows, that's a sad job, that. I don't like doing that. And mirrors. No matter how much you clean them they're still smeary at the end of it. Any dusty jobs I don't like. I don't mind hoovering. That's cool.*

WHO'S YOUR FAVOURITE RELATIVE? *My grandad, my mum's father. His name's Jim. He comes round usually once every year at Christmas. He knows what I do for a living. He's never been to a gig or anything but he watches the telly. He's a top man though. Top dude, he is.*

WHO DO YOU LOVE? *I love my mummy. I love quite a lot of people to tell you the truth. I'm not in love with them where I feel I want to be with them all the time, but I do have a lot of special friends and my family and I feel a lot of love for them. I tell them all in certain ways.*

WHAT'S YOUR MOST VIVID CHILDHOOD MEMORY? *My mum and dad's divorce. I remember that very vividly.*

WHAT'S YOUR IDEA OF PURE BLISS? *Blue sea water which is warm.*

WHO'S YOUR BEST FRIEND? *I haven't really got any best friends. I've got a few very close friends. Neil McCartney, Bradley Lincoln, Thomas Crowther, they're three of my male friends. I've got some female friends too. Not a best friend though.*

WHAT WOULD YOU DO TO MAKE THE WORLD A BETTER PLACE? *Get everybody to speak the same language. That might be nice. It might help things along.*

IS BEING A POP STAR WORTH THE TROUBLE? *Yeah, definitely.*

WHAT ARE YOU FANATICAL ABOUT? *Well I'm into curries in a big way. My addiction's getting more fierce. And my health. I'm not fanatical but I always care about my health. I dance around a lot, I swim, I do exercises, just general sports to keep me fit and I eat good food – diet is so important. I've taken a lot of stick from this lot over what I eat but they're all changing – they're all taking a leaf out of my book!*

DO YOU EVER WISH YOU DID ANOTHER JOB? *Never. No. Now and again I wish I could walk down the town and not get recognized even once, but not enough to wish I had a different job.*

IF YOU COULD CHANGE ONE THING ABOUT YOURSELF WHAT WOULD IT BE? *Erm. . .* (about six hours later) *no, there's nothing. Why? Well, I'm not happy with everything about me but it's things that I have got the power to change and I'll work on.*

WHAT COLOUR IS YOUR SOUL? *Whooh! Deep one thrown in there. That's a nice one. Erm. . .* (hours later) *don't know. Can you help me out? Are you allowed to help me? Blue? I was going to say that – blue or green. Both, I think. Kind of a darker green and blue. One of those colours. Yeah, or both. . .*

IF YOU COULD PICK A FIRST NAME FOR YOURSELF WHAT WOULD IT BE? *Dexter! haha! No, I'm only mucking about. That's a terrible name innit?! Ahahaaahhaa! That's your cat's name? Oh dear. Sorry. Um. . . Sam. Samuel. My little brother's name. That's what I'd choose.*

WHAT'S THE MOST EMBARRASSING ITEM OF CLOTHING YOU HAD TO WEAR AS A KID? *Pair of boots like these – shaped like these* (swings leg up to show brown army type things) *but with a big gold star on the side. Imagine them – this was years ago when these sort of boots hadn't even been invented. My dad told me they were gonna be fashionable and I was gonna bring them into fashion. And I believed him 'cause I thought he was dead trendy. But I didn't know he wasn't trendy at all. Shoes are important – you know if your shoes are not right you don't wanna go to school, do you?*

WHAT'S YOUR NICKNAME? *Lander, Gary invented that one.*

IF YOU WERE A JOURNALIST, WHAT QUESTION WOULD YOU ASK YOURSELF? *Erm. . . of myself? Tough question that. I don't know what I'd ask myself. When are you gonna get married?*

SO WHEN ARE YOU GOING TO GET MARRIED? *When I'm about 35 maybe, even 40. That would be ideal. I think that's when I'll be ready. I don't think most people are really ready until then.*

IF YOU COULD BE IN ANY GROUP FROM ANOTHER ERA, WHICH WOULD IT BE? *I'd love to have been in Pink Floyd* ('concept' band from the '70s and early 80s). *Yeah, they were a great band, or. . . I like Mick Jagger. In those days he had a lot – he was, like, ugly! The first ugly pop star but dead attractive, which I think is really good. He was a real character on stage.*

WHAT'S YOUR CHAT-UP LINE? *Hello, I'm Jason, what's your name?*

DO YOU THINK IT'S ALL RIGHT FOR GIRLS TO ASK BLOKES OUT? *Oh yeah, definitely. I wish there was more of it. I'd be very flattered if someone asked me out and I'd absolutely love it.*

WHAT'S YOUR FAVOURITE SANDWICH FILLING? *Tuna salad.*

WHICH QUESTION DO YOU WISH PEOPLE WOULD STOP ASKING YOU? *Any question relating to the fact that we're a pop band and that we're not gonna be around for a long time. I just think it's a question that they ask because it's the thing to ask. They haven't really gone into any depth of thought. They found out what we are - we're a pop band - and so they just ask the obvious. But you can ask any band at the moment, you could ask Guns N' Roses, 'Are you afraid of not being around for a long time?' because it's the same for everybody. It's difficult to stay around because that's the way the business is.*

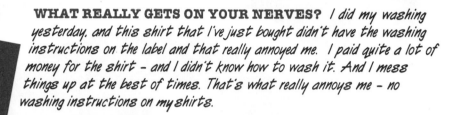

WHAT REALLY GETS ON YOUR NERVES? *I did my washing yesterday, and this shirt that I've just bought didn't have the washing instructions on the label and that really annoyed me. I paid quite a lot of money for the shirt - and I didn't know how to wash it. And I mess things up at the best of times. That's what really annoys me - no washing instructions on my shirts.*

DO YOU PRAY? *I don't pray to anybody. I pray to myself, you know, don't do this, do that, sort this out etc. I don't do it every day, just now and again.*

HAVE YOU EVER BEEN IN A SCARY SITUATION WITH A FAN? *Not really. Back in the early days when we were doing clubs it got to the point where we were getting quite big and the security wasn't able to cope with it and there were times when it got a bit hectic, so we had to do a quick dart.*

WHO DO YOU CONFIDE IN? *I confide different things to different people. I've got close friends - a close circle of friends - but I don't tell all those friends everything. I tell one person something and another person something else. I think it's my subconscious warning me not to tell people certain things because even though they're your close friends it wouldn't do you any good telling this person.*

WHAT DO YOU HATE THAT JOURNALISTS SAY ABOUT YOU? *I don't hate anything really. I dislike silly things like he's insured for five million and he's dead rich, 'cause I'm not.*

HOW DO YOU SEE YOURSELF AT 70? *My grandad, my mum's dad, is really funny. I'll phone him and I'll say, "So what you doing with yourself, Grandad, you been going out for walks or what?" He comes from down south, from London so he's, like,* (attempts really poor Cockney accent) *"Oh, my legs have packed in a bit, Jason. I can't walk." Oh, forget the accent! So I say to him, "So what do you do then, like, do you watch telly?" "Ooh, my eyes are a bit sad at the moment, J." "Oh, so do you listen to the radio then, Grandad?" "Oh, it's my ears, son. I can't listen to the radio." Haha! He must just sit there immobile all day doing nothing 'cause everything's packed up! But he's dead nice, a top man and if I'm like him when I'm 70 I'll be a happy man.*

ThE PErSonAL BiTs

Mark

WHAT'S YOUR FULL NAME? *Mark Anthony Patrick Owen.*

HOW TALL ARE YOU? *Erm, about 5'7" I'd say.*

WHERE DO YOU LIVE? *I live in Manchester with my family in an ordinary house.*

WHAT COLOUR ARE YOUR EYES? *Well, what do you think? Green? Blue? You know, we can't decide. My eyes are a funny colour. They change. I think they're more blue today.*

WHAT'S YOUR INSIDE LEG MEASUREMENT? *Erm, about 31", I think. Does that sound about right? Yeah, that must be it then.*

DO YOU WEAR BOXER SHORTS OR BRIEFS? *I don't like boxers. I prefer briefs. They're comfortable and easy. I like Calvin Kleins but I don't really care what brand they are as long as they're good ones that last.*

WHAT DO YOU DO WITH YOUR MONEY? *I spend it on little things really. My lizard, CDs, going out to the pictures, and now I've passed my driving test I'll be spending it on my car - that's if it ever goes. The first day I passed my test it broke down four times. It's knackered! Some clothes, I like clothes. Hats. . .*

WHO DO YOU LOVE? *I love my family, I suppose. I get on really well with them.*

WHAT'S YOUR WORST HOUSEHOLD CHORE? *Tidying up my bedroom. My brother is so messy and untidy it drives me mad. I'm quite a tidy person. It's got to the stage where I'm thinking of getting all the stuff he leaves on the floor and just putting it in the bin!*

WHAT'S YOUR EARLIEST CHILDHOOD MEMORY? *The first one is we had this rabbit called Snowy. He was massive, he was a like a dog. He was all white and I remember we used to let him in the house. I remember I used to sit in the front room and give him drinks out of my bottle! I'd hold my baby bottle out to his mouth and he'd suck on it and have a drink when my mum wasn't watching! I'd share a bottle with a rabbit! Ahahah!*

WHAT'S YOUR IDEA OF PURE BLISS? *Pure bliss, for me, is just to be in my bedroom listening to music or just doing my own thing in my bedroom. Lying on my own bed.*

WHO'S YOUR BEST FRIEND? *The lads, obviously. At home I've probably got three best friends. A guy called Andy, a guy called Jonathan and another guy called Phil - two from school.*

IS BEING A POP STAR WORTH THE TROUBLE? *Yeah, definitely, I would say, because of the people you meet and the things that you learn. I think maturity-wise you're learning all the time. You never stop learning: how to handle figures, how to handle your money, seeing different cultures, going to new places, seeing new cities, how people behave. Also, I've learned about determination, never letting go of your dreams, things like that. You learn without realizing that you're learning.*

WHAT ARE YOU FANATICAL ABOUT? *I'm fanatical about football. I try and play when I get the chance but I enjoy watching it. I think that's the thing. I get a lot of enjoyment out of watching it - I get a lot of emotion from it. And I really like watching local teams. Liverpool is the team I've always followed and my local team, Oldham, but I'm just a supporter of football really. I'm not a team person. If any team's doing well I'm just happy for them. I believe the best team should win.*

DO YOU EVER WISH YOU DID ANOTHER JOB? *No. I certainly don't.*

IF YOU COULD CHANGE ONE THING ABOUT YOURSELF WHAT WOULD IT BE? *My moods. Yeah, I do get moody. Sometimes I'm just in my own world and people around me talk to me and I just won't listen or hear one word. Sometimes I can be a laugh and good company to be with and at other times I can be terrible company. I can feel it sometimes. I know when I'm doing it and I try to come out of it but I can't come out of it. All I hear, right, when people talk, is like a hollow sound and I'm not really taking any notice. (Gary: I think you'd be exhausted if you didn't have those moods, Mark, you're so hyperactive.)*

IF YOU COULD PICK A FIRST NAME FOR YOURSELF WHAT WOULD IT BE? *I like Billy. I always said if I have a guy I'd like to call him Billy. Billy Joe Owen.*

WHAT'S THE MOST EMBARRASSING ITEM OF CLOTHING YOU HAD TO WEAR AS A KID? *That's difficult because when you're really young you wouldn't know. But I used to have this sort of coat called a Snorkel. It had this big hood that you pulled right forward and you couldn't see where you were going! I think they got banned because kids kept getting run over 'cause they couldn't see the cars coming when they crossed the road!*

WHAT'S YOUR NICKNAME? *Gaz made mine up. Irwin. 'Cause if you say Owen really slow – Ooooowin – it sounds like you're saying Irwin. Then Ernest came from that so I was Ernest Irwin. So I get Ern as well. (Gary: I call him Ernie now because he's driving the fastest milk cart in the west!)*

IF YOU WERE A JOURNALIST, WHAT QUESTION WOULD YOU ASK YOURSELF? *I'd ask, what do you want out of life? And the answer would be, I don't know yet.*

IF YOU COULD BE IN ANY GROUP FROM ANOTHER ERA WHICH WOULD IT BE? *Can I be one person and not in a band? I'd be Elvis. I love him. You know I wouldn't be surprised if he was still alive. Wouldn't it be good? Wouldn't it be just fantastic if they found him?*

WHAT'S YOUR CHAT-UP LINE? *I don't have a chat-up line. I like to be able to sit down and talk and see how it goes from there. Just do it naturally.*

DO YOU THINK IT'S ALL RIGHT FOR GIRLS TO ASK BLOKES OUT? *I'd like it. I think they might be a bit frightened of appearing forward but I know from a guy's point of view it would give him a lot of joy if a girl showed interest in him.*

WHAT'S YOUR FAVOURITE SANDWICH FILLING? *Tuna and salad cream on brown bread with no butter.*

WHICH QUESTION DO YOU WISH PEOPLE WOULD STOP ASKING YOU? *How does it feel being the sexiest man on earth and winning the polls. I hate that question. I don't really know how to answer it. There's nothing you can say. I just say I'm flattered. (Gary: It's like me being asked how I feel being the 7th best dressed man in The Sun. Oh yeah. I am you know. I just take it in my stride. Listen, people know class when they see it. They've got good taste. . .)*

WHAT DO YOU BELIEVE IN? *Life. I believe in everything. (Gary: You can tell he's been mixing with J lately, can't you!) Yeah! That was a Jason answer! You believe in whatever you want to believe in.*

WHAT REALLY GETS ON YOUR NERVES? *Not being able to explain myself properly. When you're trying to explain yourself and it doesn't come out right. That can happen in interviews. You're trying to get something across and it doesn't come out right and you're getting more and more annoyed inside with yourself and the more annoyed you get and the more you try to make sense the worse it goes!*

DO YOU PRAY? *I pray all the time. I pray during the day. Sometimes I can pray up to five or six times during the day. A thought'll just come in my mind, just sitting around or just about to go on stage. And I pray regularly every night too.*

WOULD YOU DO IT ALL AGAIN? *Yeah, I would. I could live this again if it was us but I couldn't if it was with somebody else. I wouldn't be able to do it alone.*

HAVE YOU EVER BEEN IN A SCARY SITUATION WITH A FAN? *It's not so much the fans; it's other people. I think we're all very wary of it. Like, you could be at the pictures with someone and you feel that somebody's watching you all the time. You feel there are always eyes on you if you're doing anything like going down a one-way street the wrong way in your car - anything - someone will see you. But I've never been threatened by a fan. I think most fans, if you try and talk to them, are fine to get on with.*

WHAT DO YOU HATE THAT JOURNALISTS SAY ABOUT YOU? *For me it's the little things that get written that can be hurtful. Say there's something in a magazine or a letter from a fan that says we're big-headed or whatever. If I feel I'm hurting somebody or people are getting the wrong impression of me through what's being written about me I don't like it.*

HOW DO YOU SEE YOURSELF WHEN YOU'RE 70? *I'd like to see myself when I'm 70 having grandchildren who I have round once a week for tea. And I'd like to go round to my sons' and daughters' houses and they come and pick me up. I'd like to see us all just getting together at Christmas and now and again. I'd like to be living in a nice little house with a wife and a dog, having a settled life.*

FANS AND THE FAN CLUB

While you've been watching Mark, Jason, Gary, Rob and Howard, they've been watching you!

Q: What's it like to receive a fan letter?

Jason: Getting a fan letter from a fan is as rewarding as getting an award at a poll. It can make you very emotional. You realize that each fan is individual, they all have problems and happiness and they are real people.

Q: Do you ever feel sad for your fans?

Howard: Sometimes I feel sorry for some of the fans because they must desperately want to get near us so much and it's so hard to get to us.

Q: How do you feel about your fans?

Mark: The fans are a part of this group. Without them we wouldn't be sitting here doing this annual. We owe so much to them.

Q: What things do your fans get up to?

Gary: They check into hotels and try to get to you any way they can! But they're never any harm and nothing bad ever happens.

Rob: Sometimes they'll ring you up in the middle of the night and say, "I can't find your house, where is it?"

Q: What does it feel like when you get stopped for an autograph?

Mark: I get embarrassed when you're walking round the local town and you get stopped and sign an autograph. You're just standing there and people keep walking past and staring!

Howard: I can get quite shy actually. When I was in Asda the other day five girls came up to me shouting 'Howard!' and I just got really shy.

Q: Describe the ideal fan.

Jason: Someone who comes to watch the show and enjoys themselves.

Rob: And who watches the videos.

Mark: And if you meet them they can be themselves.

Q: What does the fan club really do?

Gary: Well, it's run by a lady called Val, she's great. Apart from getting the newsletters, a badge, a window sticker, postcards, posters and all that stuff, you are also kept informed of what we're doing. We answer as many letters as we can but these days we're always travelling and there are so many letters it would be impossible to answer them all.

Mark: But we do read as many as we can and Val sorts out the ones we should answer personally. And she's always keeping us informed about what the fans are asking and what they want.

Rob: It's our lifeline to the fans – it's like a big party telephone line – we can tell them about us and they can tell us about them.

Jason: Also there are lots of offers on T-shirts and other merchandise that you can't buy in the shops.

Howard: I think we'd all like to take this opportunity to say a big THANK YOU to everyone for supporting us and to each and every member of the fan club.

Thank you, thank you, thank you. . .

JOIN UP!

If you're one of the three people left in the entire world who isn't a member of the Official Take That Fan Club and you fancy joining, they'll be happy to hear from you. Write to:

Val
The Take That Fan Club
P.O. Box 538
Manchester
M60 2DX

And she'll get you sorted!

TAKE THAT

TAKE THAT ANSWER BACK!

Mark, Gary, Howard, Rob and Jason receive thousands of questions from you every week. Here they answer a few of their favourite ones. Bet you wish you'd never asked now!

DO YOU PUT YOUR TOWEL ON THE RADIATOR SO IT'S NICE AND WARM FOR WHEN YOU GET OUT OF THE SHOWER?

Howard: I haven't got a radiator in my bathroom so the answer is no.

Mark: I do.

Jason: I put mine on the toilet seat so I can reach it when I get out of the bath.

Gary: I hang it on the radiator.

Jason: Rob wears his towel round him in the shower so he doesn't have to do it when he gets out!

Rob: I wear it in the bath too, saves time later!

HAVE YOU EVER DONE ANYTHING YOU REGRET?

Howard: Yeah, I stole a packet of sweets from a shop when I was about 15. I remember nicking them, going to my grandad's, hiding and then finally going home and there was a policeman there and I got slapped round the room!

Rob: I nicked Mark Hassel's ruler when I was at school. I was only six and Mr Collins slapped me. I had a spate of pinching car signs from cars, too. I nicked this BMW car sign once and I got guilty so I went to the pub and told the fella I'd nicked it and gave it back.

Howard: I also nicked something out of Gary's room – a sample CD, but I never told him.

Gary: Oh right, now it's all coming out. . . Jason's got one to own up for but he won't tell you.

Jason: No, I'm not telling that one, sorry.

Howard: I think we all nick things from each other's rooms but only in jest – we think it's quite funny!

Gary: Remember when I nicked your credit card, J? He'd only had it one day and I nicked his Visa!

WHICH IS BETTER, A BATH OR A SHOWER?

Howard: The bath, although I have more showers than baths due to lack of time but a bath is more relaxing and luxurious.

Mark: I use a bath as a treat every now and then. I usually have a shower because I haven't got time.

Robbie: I have a bath because you can lie in your own water then.

Gary: I prefer a shower because I feel cleaner when I get out the shower.

Jason: I have a bath to relax and a shower to follow. I'm in there for ages!

Mark: That's why it takes him so long to come to the door!

Howard: Yeah, have you noticed that? We'll be in a hotel and you'll knock on J's door and it takes him ages to come to the door.

Mark: And then when he does come to the door he's got no clothes on and he's just standing there!

Howard: He gets out of the bath, has a shave and gets back in there for another 20 minutes!

DO YOU HAVE ANY SCARS?

Howard: Yeah my eyebrow, and I've got one right on the inside of my leg right at the top. When I was young I had a boil there. I've got a scar on my head as well. I had to have twelve stitches in my head. I jumped off this kitchen table in a play centre and hit my head on this steel girder.

Rob: I've got a scar on my leg from when all the kids went swimming in the reservoir. What had happened was a piece of metal had got caught in my leg and I got dragged down and it had split my leg.

Gary: I've got one on my cheek from when I did a karate demonstration and I got hit by a flying knife.

Mark: I've got one on the side of my face from when I fell off my BMX from when I was nine or ten. And my knees are very scarred from playing football.

Jason: I've got one under my eye – I just fell over – one on my stomach from falling off a fence and I've got a scar on my groin from a hernia operation I had a few years ago. And one on my foot from playing sports.

DO YOU SUFFER FROM FOOT ODOUR?

(Everyone looks at Rob and laughs!)

Gary: I don't think any of us have. (The others agree.)

Rob: I had a foot odour problem which lasted a year and a half from wearing the same trainers without socks, OK?

DID YOU HAVE SCHOOL DINNERS OR A GIRLIE PACKED LUNCH?

Gary: Packed lunch.

Jason: School dinner.

Howard: I had free school dinners.

Mark: School dinners. I had the same dinner for about the last three years – chips, beans and brown sauce.

Gary: I always used to have a Mars Bar every day at school and my mate's mum used to give him a Mars Bar too and we used to see who could eat it the quickest. A Mars Bar race! By the time you'd pushed it all in you couldn't chew and it'd all be dripping out your mouth! They're dead chewy as well are Mars Bars, it was dead difficult.

Rob: I had a mixture of both school dinners and packed lunches and everybody else's leftovers!

WHEN WAS THE LAST TIME YOU GOT ON A BUS OR OTHER PUBLIC TRANSPORT?

Jason: About four weeks ago, I was going into town.

Howard: Mine was about two months ago. I went up to Gary's on the train.

Rob: I'm always going on the train, whenever I come into Manchester to meet the lads I always get the train back to Stoke.

Gary: I've only ever been on a bus twice – once when I went to get my car back from being serviced and one time Howard dragged me on a bus – from his house into town.

Mark: I went on a bus about a week ago when I went to my local town centre.

WERE YOU EVER A PREFECT AT SCHOOL?

Gary: I was the bell ringer once – you know when you ring the bell at break? Yeah that was me.

Howard: Our prefects got hassled at our school, just for being a prefect really.

Rob: No, it wasn't cool to be a prefect – not saying that I was hip at school because I wasn't.

Mark: At junior school I was head of our house, Arrowsmith.

Jason: Yeah I was head of Greenfinch for the whole year.

Gary: I was the head of Eton House.

Rob: I was junior captain of the golf club.

Howard: Oh, it's all coming out now. . .

DID YOU EVER GET DETENTION AT SCHOOL?

Howard: Yeah, I caused a lot of detentions for my whole class. Not through anything really stupid, just through not doing my work and throwing things about or when you used to line up outside the classroom we used to have this stupid game where everyone at the back of the line would push everyone forward and crush everyone in the corner.

Rob: I used to get detention. I took the rap for things.

Howard: What do you mean, like you were a mean rapper at school? (Everyone else sniggers at this.)

Rob: Yeah! Yo teacher don't gimme a detention, don't talk I won't mention. . . I'd get detentions for not doing homework, for being loud in class. . . I used to get sent to the top man quite often.

Gary: I did get detention once (everyone looks surprised). I was playing the drums in the music room right next to the examining hall and they were doing A levels in there so I got detention for that.

Mark: I got detention at school basically for just things like not doing homework, laughing and giggling in class, being late back into class for registration.

Jason: Yeah I got detention. I was mates with some lads and one of them would always tell these really funny jokes and we'd all laugh and when the teacher turned round they were able to stop laughing and I couldn't hold it in.

Howard: I got the cane about seven times and the slipper twice.

WHAT'S THE ONE THING YOU'D HATE TO LOSE?

Howard: My mother.

Gary: Good call.

Jason: Yeah my mum. . . my bone beads because I always wear them and I'd hate to lose them.

Mark: I hate losing anything. I suppose I'm quite superstitious about losing anything. I give lives to things. I remember when I was a kid I'd give a life to even little things that I didn't particularly like, if I had a drink out of a can that can would have a life and I shouldn't put it in the bin, I'd bring it home. And grass – if I stood on grass – don't kill the grass!

Howard: (Putting on 'hard' face) I was like that but I wasn't as kiddish about it, all that going on about lives and things. I was much more hard! I bought things like toffee papers and never threw them away because I thought I'd miss them.

Rob: I keep things in my pockets because I can't drop things. Dropping litter is disgusting.

Howard: I tell you who's the worst litter bug: Gary. Sorry to bring that up but you are.

Rob: Of course I wouldn't like to lose my mum but there's a few jackets I'd want to hang on to.

Gary: No, they joke about my wallet but see this (gets out wallet) it's leather and it's got GB in the corner and it was given to me by a fan and it's beautiful. I'd never want to lose it.

Mark: And cards as well, I keep them.

DO YOU SQUEEZE THE TOOTHPASTE FROM THE BOTTOM OR FROM THE MIDDLE OF THE TUBE?

Howard: Bottom.

Mark: Yeah, from the bottom.

Jason: If I get a new tube I start at the bottom but then I sack it and just squeeze it anywhere.

Gary: I roll it, get every last drop then I cut it open! Listen, I tell you what, it's dear gear that toothpaste! (By now the others are cracking up. And an intense discussion is under way to determine how to make the most of your toothpaste!)

Rob: God, I have never seen these lads so enthusiastic over a question. It's only toothpaste. Do you know what though, I have a pump dispenser because it's big and cumbersome and it's difficult to leave in places because you can always see it!

WHAT WAS THE LAST TOILETRY ITEM YOU BOUGHT?

Gary: Toilet rolls – yesterday – I had to smuggle them in the house past the fans! And baby lotion.

Howard: Neutrogena moisturiser.

Rob: Oh yeah, I got some Neutrogena the other day.

Mark: Yeah, me too.

Jason: Can't remember what the very last thing was but I did buy some Neutrogena moisturiser recently too. Eh, lads, perhaps we'll get some free now – I mean we're all using it and it's dead expensive.

HOW MANY FILLINGS HAVE YOU GOT?

Howard: About four fillings.

Rob: Two.

Gary: I reckon I've got about six.

Mark: One.

Jason: Three.

WHICH BRAND OF DEODORANT DO YOU USE?

Jason: I don't use deodorant.

Howard: Yeah but you are gonna start using it, aren't you, mate?

Jason: No, I haven't used it yet.

Howard: But you said you were going to because you were sweating really badly and you stank.

Mark: Yeah your mum told you you smelled didn't she?!

Jason: Yeah, thanks lads. I don't use deodorant. I never have done and I never will do. I wash every day and there's no need to use it.

Mark: When I feel I need it I use Natrel.

Gary: I have actually got quite a collection that fans have sent me, so I'll wear anything. Your armpits do get smelly no matter what. And let me be the one to tell you Lander (i.e. Jason) yours too. You wanna get some aerosol under your pits.

Rob: I use a stick – just anything my mum gets in.

Howard: I don't use any particular type but I got one for Christmas called Journey.

DO YOU USE DENTAL FLOSS?

Gary: I've only just started using that, funny stuff innit?

Howard: I've only ever used it once and that was on a plane 'cause you got it free.

Jason: I use it sometimes.

Mark: Again, like J, I use it if I remember.

Rob: No, no, I'm sorry I don't. Brushing is enough innit?

JASON ORANGE

Describe your mum.

"I like talking about my mum. She's the best, she's absolutely beautiful looking. She's kind, caring – very kind, very caring and she'd always put us before herself."

What does your mum think of you being famous?

"She absolutely loves it. She revels in it. Sometimes I have to slow her down, say 'Look, calm down a bit.' She's just really happy and she's very proud."

Do you think she worries about you?

"Yeah. I think she worries about whether I'm eating properly, whether I'm getting enough sleep, whether I'm working too hard, whether I'm happy or not. She's always saying, 'Jason, are you happy?'"

Does she still tell you off?

"I haven't been told off by my mum for a long time. When I'm at home we're just like two mates rather than mother and son. But I'm sure she would tell me off if she had reason to."

Were you a good baby?

"When I was a baby, myself and Justin – the twins – used to set each other off. If I was happy he was happy and if one of us started crying the other one felt he had to cry to get the attention."

Did she ever have to go up to school?

"No, she never came up to school. I always used to sort things out before it got to that stage."

Did you help round the house?

"I always used to do things to help my mum round the house when I was little because I knew she was bringing us all up on her own and I was sensitive to that at quite an early age."

JASON'S MUM, JENNY

Describe your son.

"He's very special, he's very kind and thoughtful, he's very caring and he's got quite a lot of understanding of people."

What do you think of him being famous?

"I'm really proud of him, he's worked hard to get where he is."

Do you worry about him?

"There are a few things I'm scared of. I worry about him flying everywhere. We're both bad flyers and I feel nervous when he's in the air. I used to worry if he was getting enough rest. I hope he's eating well – he usually eats quite sensibly. He's usually got a bag of nuts and raisins on him."

Do you think he worries about you?

"Probably. I think he worries that I work too hard. He's said a couple of times, 'You all right, Mum? I worry about you.' "

Do you still tell him off?

"No. I don't think so. I don't remember the last time. But if I had a reason to tell him off I'd tell him, all right!"

What do you nag him about?

"I do nag him a bit about food – he does look a bit thin, and it worries me."

Was he a good kid?

"Yeah. He's a twin, as you know, and I remember, with him and Justin being together, if you ever went to the loo or had a shower they'd always be sitting outside knocking on the door yelling, 'Mum! Mum!' But they kept each other occupied, they seemed to have their own language."

Did he help round the house?

"Yeah he did. I think they all did, they had to do their bit what with me having six. He's very mature but they all had their mad moments – even Jason!"

Describe your mum.

"I think she looks like Demi Moore. She's very caring and very loving. I think my mum is probably the father figure in our house as well, even though my dad won't like me saying so!"

What does she think of you being famous?

"She enjoys it but I think she's always concerned for me."

Does she worry about you?

"The slightest thing will set her off. I think she's worried that we'll lose the fans a lot of the time, she's always saying the fans are the ones who got you there in the first place. She worries when we're away from home for too long and she worries about me not eating."

Do you worry about her?

"I worry about her being overworked and over stressed."

Does she still tell you off?

"About my bedroom, yeah. . .she doesn't tell me off, she doesn't shout, she'll just say, 'That bedroom's looking a mess'."

What does she nag you about?

"She gets uptight about the lizard. She thinks it stinks! When I bought it home she took it a lot better than I thought she would, I thought she'd die. I know she has a soft spot for it really."

Did you help around the house?

"I was playing the eldest role and giving an example to our Tracey and Daniel. I was always helping my mum out with the shopping, helping to clean up and I'd shout at Daniel and Tracey to come and clean up."

Were you a good baby?

"You'll have to ask my mum. I think I was the one who cried."

Did she have to go up to school?

"No, she was never called into school or anything, no letters home or anything terrible on my report."

Describe your son.

"Well, he's very bubbly, he doesn't keep things in, he takes a lot of pride in himself. And he does worry a lot."

What do you think of him being famous?

"I'm proud of him, obviously. He's just a normal lad really, like last week we went shopping and he was singing and messing about in the store, he still has his little games of football, he does his own little shopping, he's exactly the same."

Do you worry about him?

"Oh yeah, I do. With him being on the road with things like these road accidents. And I worry whether he's eating properly. I worry he'll be pulled off stage."

Do you think he worries about you?

"Yeah, if I'm that little bit ill he always rings up from wherever he is. And he nags me, he says, 'Don't go to work tomorrow, Mum, if you feel tired.' He's really good like that."

Do you still tell him off?

"I don't really have to. It's just his clothes, he's got about three suitcases of clothes upstairs and they're all just piled on top of each other. It's a wonder he can find his clothes half the time so I just tidy them up a bit for him but I don't tell him off."

What do you nag him about?

"The lizard. I can't stand that. But I sprayed it with furniture polish once by accident and I thought I'd killed it. I went in my bedroom and cried and cried!"

Did he help around the house?

"Now he does, yes, but when he was little he more or less damaged the house rather than helped out with it. He always had a ball at his feet. I remember once we were putting a window in at the front and his ball came in through the window at the back! He was football mad – he still is."

Was he a good baby?

"He was a good baby. He always used to be sick! When he was first born he was brought up on cornflour just to put a lining on his stomach."

Did you ever go up to school?

"No, he always had good reports."

MARK'S MUM, MARY

ROBBIE WILLIAMS

Describe your mum.

"My mum is wonderful. And she's got all the answers to everything. My mum's very, very wise and can sort my problems out. She's a very beautiful person."

Do you worry about her?

"She's looking after so many people at any one time, helping them out, that she doesn't look after her own interests and that bothers me."

What does she think of you being famous?

"My mum's quite happy for me to be doing anything, really. As long as I'm achieving and getting off my backside."

Does she worry about you?

"Yeah, oh god yeah. Unlike the others' mums she never worries if I'm eating right because she knows I'm always eating right! As long as I've got my personal life sorted out then she's fine."

Does she still tell you off?

"Yeah, I got a telling off last night for losing my wallet."

What does she nag you about?

"She nags me just because I'm lazy and forgetful, the normal things."

Were you a good kid?

"I was quite cocky – never to the point where anyone would think, I'm not having Jan round because her son's a twit. I was never impolite and always very thankful."

Did she ever have to go up to school?

"No, I was cheeky but not really bad."

Did you help around the house?

"No, I was very, very lazy. She told me off all the time – it would come to blows – I mean she would come to blows with me! I was very, very lazy and I still am."

Describe your son.

"A good son, caring, thoughtful – always carried the neighbours' shopping – never raises his voice to me. His manners have always been good. He's always happy, a pleasure to have around."

Do you think he worries about you?

"The first thing Robert does when he comes in is to look at my face to see how I am. His face lights up if mine's OK."

What do you think about him being famous?

"I worry about it. I worry about his safety. I worry about drugs, drink, being pulled into situations that you get in a different financial bracket. On top of that I worry about the fans and their heartaches and I know Robert does too."

Do you worry about him?

"I worry about him leaving everything everywhere. His head must be in the shed but having said that he's always been like it. Every week I was always having to have a new key cut for him because he'd manage to lose it."

Do you still tell him off?

"Yes I do. I just say, 'I want you in the office' – that's what I call it when he needs a talking to. His bedroom's always in a state and I tell him I am not here to wait on him hand and foot!"

What do you nag him about?

"Being careless with his possessions and his Barclaycard."

Was he a good kid?

"Well, he didn't do his homework and odd little things."

Did you ever go up to school?

"I had to go up and see the head about his homework and different little things but nothing terrible like stealing or bullying."

Did he help around the house?

"Oh god! Well, if you asked him to do anything he would try, but I could guarantee that in trying he would either burn the house down or create such a huge problem that it was easier just to sort it out myself."

ROB'S MUM, JAN

HOWARD DONALD

Describe your mum.

"My mummy. . . she's very sensitive. . . she's so lovely. . . she supported me in the beginning. One day I really want to spoil her just to say thanks, Mum, for, you know, for being my mother really."

Does she worry about you?

"She's quite a worrier about what I do. She worries when I come in off the road and I don't sit down and talk to her – she thinks something's wrong or she thinks she's done something wrong."

Do you worry about her?

"Erm. . . I don't really, no. Because I think she can look after herself. She's good at that. And she's got a good husband, Mike, my stepdad."

Does she still tell you off?

"She never shouts at me but little things like, 'Don't park your car in front of the house next door,' or 'Don't leave your equipment on in your room.'"

Were you a good kid?

"I was, actually. I think when I was 13 or 14 I started getting into mischief."

Were you a good baby?

"She says I was the best behaved. I was the one she didn't have to bother with as much as the rest of them."

Did she have to go up to school?

"(Laughs) Yeah, there was a lot of times my mum was embarrassed because of me – more of my work than being naughty. I didn't like school much and I suppose that's why I played truant for about seven weeks."

Did you help around the house?

"No. I feel a bit guilty about it because I'm sure my mum could have done with the support a lot of the time. She's a wonderful lady and she's attractive for her age and I think she'd be more attractive if she wasn't put under such stress."

Describe your son.

"He's very loving. He'll come to me and tell me everything, so I always feel quite close to him. He's very honest, too – he's not afraid to say what he thinks but he won't say anything nasty. He tries to help people, he's very good like that."

Do you worry about him?

"One minute I think their success is absolutely wonderful, the next I'm frightened in case the bubble bursts. I can't take it but I know he could. If he has disappointments in life he can ride them, he'll just say, 'What are you worried about Mum? It's just got to be.'"

Do you think he worries about you?

"He worries for me when the fans come round if they cause a lot of trouble and when my youngest is being cheeky Howard will say, 'Don't you be cheeky to my mum!' He gets very annoyed."

Do you still tell him off?

"Oh yes, about his room because it's like a pigsty. And he leaves his underwear on the bathroom floor!"

Was he a good kid?

"Well, he was naughty, he didn't get in serious trouble but he was a wonderful baby. When he was teenager he got a bit naughty."

Was he a good baby?

"When he was a baby his father wouldn't mind him because he kept throwing his bottle out of his cot!"

Did you have to go up to school?

"I only went once because some bigger boys were fighting him. He was always very small for his age up until he was about 17."

Did he help around the house?

"No! In fact the only time he's ever done anything was this year when we went on holiday. He actually went shopping to Asda and cooked himself a meal for the first time! But I still came back to a pile of pots in the sink! I think he's only ever washed up about twice in his life. He ran a few errands but only if there were some toffees in it."

HOWARD'S MUM, CATH

Describe your mum.

"*Small, red hair. . . the old man says never marry a woman with red hair – he married the old lady! No she's great is my mum. Been behind me all the way.*"

What does your mum think of you being famous?

"*She loves it – apart from the constant phone calls to the house. When she has visitors she has to take the phone off the hook. I think she's actually very happy for me.*"

Do you think she worries about you?

"*Yeah, definitely. I think she worries too much. I think she's worried I'll get involved with the wrong people. I think she's aware that this business can be quite cut throat.*"

Do you worry about her?

"*All the time. I worry about her, actually, because she doesn't chill out at any time. I'd like her to relax more.*"

Were you good at school?

"*I was a brat at school! I just knew it all, honestly. And I was a bit of a ringleader: 'This is wrong, children! We must get on to it!' This is when I was about seven! 'We must go on strike!' I was one of them! Real trouble maker!*"

Does she still tell you off?

"*No.*"

What does she nag you about?

"*My mum doesn't really nag me about anything actually. She's quite sensitive, my mum, she doesn't like to have bad words with me because she gets really upset.*"

What were you like as a baby?

"*I was bad crier! They had to call the nurse one day 'cause I was crying so much. I don't know why I was crying – I just fancied it. Says it all, that, dunnit?*"

Did you help around the house?

"*No, I was lazy, like everyone else.*"

Were you a good kid?

"*Yeah, I was the good one out the two of us – my brother was always the bad one, always in trouble and I was the real goody one!*"

Describe your son.

"*He's always been very ambitious. Exceedingly good in comparison to his brother, who was a little horror. Always wanting to please. Whatever he took up he made sure he did it very, very well. He very rarely gives up.*"

What do you think of him being famous?

"*I wouldn't say it's all wonderful. I haven't really let it reach my brain, I don't think. I think that's the way I'm dealing with it. Of course, I'm very proud of what he's achieved.*"

Do you worry about him?

"*Yes, a lot. I worry about him changing too much – I'd hate him to do that. I'd like to be a bit more a part of what he does but you've got to let them get on and go on their own little way.*"

Do you think he worries about you?

"*No, he doesn't have to, his dad's here, I've got plenty of support. He's no need to worry. I'll be here when he's finished and comes back.*"

Was he good at school?

"*Very good until the third year when the third year head stopped me and told me he was on report. And that was the first time that the good little Gary was altering slightly.*"

Do you still tell him off?

"*No, not really.*"

Nothing you nag him about?

"*Oh, no.*"

Was he a good baby?

"*He was a terrible crier. I had to fetch the health visitor to see if she could help me but she couldn't find anything wrong with him. But we sat it out and we won!*"

Did he help round the house?

"*No. He was lazy but I was a fool. I just did it.*"

Was he a good kid?

"*He was. Quite a wanter, though. You'd be frightened to take him into Chester shopping because he'd be straight in Rutherfords the organ shop and he'd always persuade you to buy him a new keyboard! It cost us a fortune!*"

GARY'S MUM, MARGE

tHE PErsonal Bits

Gary

THE SCENE:
We do this interview sitting on two steps in Take That's manager Nigel Martin-Smith's house. It's in the lounge. Gary is lying down on the top step, swigging a bottle of Evian Water. He's wearing black Katherine Hamnett jeans, an old navy and red T-shirt that's a cast off from Robbie and his black canvas shoes from Next. Half way through the interview, Mark wanders over to listen in and add a few comments of his own.

WHAT'S YOUR FULL NAME? *Gary Barlow.*

HOW TALL ARE YOU? *Around about 5'9" or 5'10", I suppose.*

WHERE DO YOU LIVE? *I've got a house just outside Manchester where I live on my own with my grandfather clock!*

WHAT COLOUR EYES DO YOU HAVE? *Blue.*

WHAT'S YOUR INSIDE LEG MEASUREMENT? *I'd say about 32". I'll tell you, I never used to worry about my height or think I was short until I started to work with them three over there* (nods his head towards Howard, Rob and Jason who are sitting on a sofa nearby). *Them six footers. They're all so tall! It's not natural. But you're always gonna feel short standing next to them, aren't ya?*

DO YOU WEAR BOXER SHORTS OR BRIEFS? *Briefs. I don't like boxers. I'm loath to say where I get my underpants from because this lot'll start on at me. I do wear Calvins, I'm not that tight, but I like them multi packs from British Home Stores best, five pairs for a tenner. That's good value for money.*

WHAT DO YOU SPEND YOUR MONEY ON? *Well, I buy a lot of equipment. I bought a piano, I want to get a baby grand for my house. I spend money on getting my house done up. I'm having an extension built. I went down to IKEA the other day and bought some lovely cutlery. . .*

WHO DO YOU LOVE? *I love the guys in the band, I suppose. It's amazing how close we've all become, over the past year especially. We all got on well before but it's really come together, so much so that I think we're at the stage that if any of us left we'd suffer – I mean personally as well as professionally. We all need each other and if one of us isn't there it really feels like someone's missing, that things aren't complete.*

WHAT'S YOUR WORST HOUSEHOLD CHORE? *Cleaning the toilet. I hate that job. It doesn't matter that it's your own toilet and you always keep it clean, it's still revolting.*

WHAT'S YOUR IDEA OF PURE BLISS? (Adopts grandad voice) *Ah, winding the old grandfather clock. . . no, pure bliss is to go home and know I've got a week off and I can sit in my studio and write songs.*

WHO'S YOUR BEST FRIEND? *All the lads really. Yeah, they're my best friends. But my best friend outside the band is called Paul. I've known him all my life.*

IS BEING A POP STAR WORTH THE TROUBLE? *Yeah, every bit of it, because of the things you get to do, the tours, the records you get to make, the places you get to see.*

WHAT ARE YOU FANATICAL ABOUT? *My breakfast. I'm fanatical about my breakfast. I do like to bake my homemade Pillsbury Dough croissants but I'm not particularly fanatical about those. If I don't get at least toast and cornflakes I'm not happy. I need to start the day well. If I don't get them I know it's gonna be a rotten day.*

DO YOU EVER WISH YOU HAD ANOTHER JOB? *No.*

WHO'S YOUR FAVOURITE RELATIVE? *I haven't got one.*

IF YOU COULD CHANGE ONE THING ABOUT YOURSELF WHAT WOULD IT BE? *Probably my undies! No, erm. . .I wish I was taller. I'm not particularly short but like I said, it's being with them three. It doesn't help. It's awful, innit, Mark?* (Mark is sitting by us now listening to Gary's answers.) *It's not on. It doesn't look right.* Mark: *They stand out a mile, I think. I feel sorry for 'em.*

IF YOU COULD PICK A FIRST NAME FOR YOURSELF WHAT WOULD IT BE? *I'm happy with mine actually. Gary.*

WHAT WAS THE MOST EMBARRASSING ITEM OF CLOTHING YOU HAD TO WEAR AS A KID? *A tank top. It was like, you know, like those horrible golfing trousers? That sort of design. It was cream with horrible lines across it. It was terrible, I hated it. It was something my mum bought me and I had to wear it.*

WHAT'S YOUR NICKNAME? *Lander.* (Mark, chipping in: *Or Barry.* Gary: *No, don't put that. Don't put that, please!* Mark: *I think you should.* Gary: *No don't, please.*) *Lander, mine is. Me and J share the same one. You see I was watching The Highlander and Jason's middle name is Thomas - we used to call him J T Orange - and so I started calling him the T Lander. And because I was GB, I was the B Lander and it went on from there.* (Eh?) *Daft, innit?*

IF YOU WERE A JOURNALIST, WHICH QUESTION WOULD YOU ASK YOURSELF? *I'd probably ask 'Would you ever move from England?' I don't think I've ever been asked that. I would move from England. I haven't seen anywhere else I'd like to live yet, though, but as soon as I do see somewhere I'll go because it's the weather I don't like. I think if you can live in a hot country why bother with England? Know what I mean?*

IF YOU COULD BE IN ANY GROUP FROM ANOTHER ERA WHICH WOULD IT BE? *Mine would be The Beatles. Mm. I'd have been George Harrison - he's my least favourite really - because then I would have been working with Paul McCartney. I'd have probably sacked the drummer and got a new one.*

WHAT'S YOUR CHAT-UP LINE? *I don't chat-up. No, never. I'm not too shy, I just don't. I think a look can start something off. You catch someone's eye and it goes from there.*

DO YOU THINK IT'S All RIGHT FOR GIRLS TO ASK BLOKES OUT? *Oh aye. I like it best when they start to talk first anyway. That way a lot of girls would be less hassled by guys they don't want to talk to. I feel really sorry for girls. Girls get hassled all the time, don't they? It must be murder.*

WHAT'S YOUR FAVOURITE SANDWICH FILLING? *Chicken. Just on its own. No mayonnaise. Just chicken on brown bread and butter. Yes, lovely.*

WHICH QUESTION DO YOU WISH PEOPLE WOULD STOP ASKING YOU? *How did the group get started? I hate people asking that. It's so boring and so complicated so you have to go through it all. It wasn't just a case of putting an advert in a magazine and looking for band members, there's a whole story and you've got to tell it all and it just takes ages. And people still keep on asking it.*

WHAT DO YOU BELIEVE IN? *I believe in myself. I just do. If I didn't believe in what I did then I probably wouldn't be able to do it as well as I do. I have to believe that I can do a vocal performance, that I can go on TV and do a live vocal, that sort of thing.*

CAN YOU COOK? *Now you're asking! Now you're asking the right sort of questions! Can I cook? Can I cook?! I can cook anything: Korma, Italian, home made soups, desserts. I'm an excellent cook. When I get in that kitchen it's like magic. I like my food. But basically, anything that's on the shelves in Tesco's I can turn into something. Oh yes.*

WHAT GETS ON YOUR NERVES? *I hate it when people watch you when you're shopping. That really bugs me. You know, when people try and see what's in your trolley, that bugs me that - it really bugs me.*

DO YOU PRAY? *Yeah. I pray. Every night. I just say things like, 'Keep people safe and make tomorrow a good day, please let me write a hit record.' You know. Yes, I do. I do pray for hit records!*

WOULD YOU DO IT ALL AGAIN? *Mm, yeah. Certainly. But I think if the band stopped and I got a chance to be in another band then I wouldn't do it all again. I'd only do this situation again. It wouldn't be the same if we did it with other people.*

HAVE YOU EVER BEEN IN A SCARY SITUATION WITH A FAN? *No, never. I think other people worry about us more than we do. We never see anybody as a threat to us.*

WHAT DO YOU HATE THAT JOURNALISTS SAY ABOUT YOU? *I hate it when they say or write anything bad. I hate bad things being written. Things like how I'm losing millions of pounds in court cases and other lies. It's just daft, it's misinforming people.*

HOW DO YOU SEE YOURSELF WHEN YOU'RE 70? *Dunno. I just hope that I'm happy when I'm 70. I hope I've had a few kids and I've got them to carry on what I've been doing. Would I encourage them to be pop stars? Yes, no doubt about it. It's a brilliant job.*

Aliens have landed!

More Aliens land.

SNAP HAPPY!

OVER THE LAST FEW MONTHS, TAKE THAT HAVE TAKEN A POLAROID CAMERA WITH THEM EVERYWHERE THEY'VE BEEN TO CAPTURE THEIR BEST MEMORIES. HERE ARE THEIR FAVOURITES...

Aliens learning
Earth language

Aliens attempt to
communicate with
Earthlings...

Captain Orange – The Thunder in America

At a photo shooter for us Mag in Denmark

o took this one?

Doing a radio show called "The Voice". Nice smile Dougie.

At the fair in Denmark – before the rollercoaster.

They won't be smiling in a minute... The fair in Denmark

Reading foreign press on a plane to Europe

"Ere, gerrof my piano!" Singing live on European Radio.

Meeting some fans – and they're all shorter than me!

I'll kill him & be the lead singer!

On a rooftop in America with some rad people!

Amsterdam airport. Clock the new sweatshirt!

J, limbering up for the gig in Denmark

Bob: Doesn't anyone want my autograph?

Gaz in his new job at the local record shop!

Nice looking girl, that!

Taken by Mark who then was told to bog off so I could get in the kid!

Doing a gig in Denmark on a small stage Jason

"Honest - we haven't had a drop of drink."

'Kre lods, how does our new one go?

At a record signing in Denmark.

At a photo Shoot in NYK just Scribbing in me diary

Me and Gary kipping
Me and Gary kipping
Me and Gary kipping.

Getting ready for a photoshoot in NYK

So, 'ave you got any Banoffi pie in the fridge? Gaz looking for food in NYK.

On the way to a gig in Denmark - look we match the plane!

Jason with some Orange. Ho ho ho!!

Yes, it's me. And I am a big lad, thanks.

SPILLING THE BEANZ!

Take That talk behind each other's backs!

THE OTHERS ON ROBBIE

Gary: Rob's very talented although he doesn't utilise his talent. He doesn't better it – he just opens his mouth and expects this fantastic voice to emerge. And he has got a much better voice than I have – he could have a fantastic voice if he tried. He's one of these people who was just born talented.

Howard: He makes you sick when you go into the studio and he hasn't been practising and he opens his mouth and it's perfect!

Mark: His mind wanders a lot. He can only concentrate on something for a short amount of time and then he'll drift. Even though he and I hang around together a lot I don't think I know him better than the others.

Howard: But you are best mates aren't you, leaving us out!

Mark: You can say loads about Rob, he's obviously the funny one, very cheeky. And he can be very fast – he can come back with comments and quips straight away, sometimes he talks without thinking. He keeps us laughing.

Howard: When I was his age I was a lot more immature than him – so I think compared to me he's mature.

Jason: It's the other way for me. When I was 19 I was more responsible than Rob and that's part of his charm – he's a little boy lost.

Mark: I think he's very emotional and I think he hides a lot of what he feels sometimes.

Howard: I think Rob's the sweetest in the band – he's an innocent.

THE OTHERS ON JASON

Gary: I think Lander's funny, sensitive. . .

Rob: He's a right character in the band.

Gary: He's really serious about life and he reckons he shrugs it off but he doesn't. Even when he's eating a yoghurt he's really serious about eating it. Everything he does he has to think about it ten times before he does it – especially when he's spending money!

Howard: A lot of fans think that Mark's the cutest – I don't think he is, I think Jason's the cutest – there's a difference between being sweet which Mark is and cute which Jason is. He's cute because he plays his guitar and he's so interested in it – and the way he concentrates he looks dead cute. I'm not soft really, I'm quite hard!

Gary: When us four are in the room together having a laugh – even though you're having a great time – you know when one's missing and you miss J more than anyone else.

Rob: Because J really laughs at our jokes!

Mark: He's very aware. One thing is he does worry and things stick in his mind. If he's got something on his mind he'll lock himself away and he won't talk to anyone about it. He won't say how he feels until he's ready. It's so apparent when he's not happy.

Gary: If I was to put J in a public position I'd have him as leader of the Labour Party. Honestly, that's where all his views lie. I think he'd make a good councillor. He's very caring.

Jason: I think Gary should actually be an ostrich. Ostriches are just such eccentric animals and they do silly things like bury their heads in the sand and walk around sticking their bums out! And they always know where the water is. Gaz always knows which side his bread's buttered. He has an unusual sense about which direction to go. He doesn't say much about where he's going but he knows he's going there.

Mark: And he goes there quietly.

Howard: He's a very sarcastic person.

Jason: A lot of the time he's sarcastic it's to make us laugh – none of it's malicious. He's witty. He thinks up nicknames for us all and he has a good way of taking the mickey out of us all.

Rob: Gaz is just the boy next door! Sometimes he does good cooking and that. When you stay at his house he puts you up nice and proper.

Jason: The big thing with Gaz is he's smart.

Mark: He knows his eggs from his chickens.

Jason: If we're under pressure it's good to have Gaz there – I don't think he sees himself as a leader but he is actually quite a leader and if there's a decision to be made we all turn to Gaz and subconsciously we wait for him to speak and when he does speak he's quite right.

THE OTHERS ON MARK

Gary: I did a little studio session at my house recently with Mark and I think I got to know him more that night than ever before. He really doesn't believe in himself at all. Not on the singing front – he doesn't know how nice a voice he's got. He's very polite and very well brought up.

Rob: Very polite and very caring – he cares a lot.

Jason: I don't think you can say one bad thing about Mark. There are not a lot of people in the world like that. He's not perfect a lot of the time and he's insecure and sometimes that comes out as aggression but, you know, it's nothing bad inside him.

Rob: He's a bit heavy handed. And he runs like a bullet!

Howard: He's very committed like Jason is and, as Gaz says, you get to know him more when you're on your own rather than with the group. He cares about himself a lot – in the way that he looks as in fashion.

Gary: He's a bit of a follower is Mark. That's not a bad thing but I think in the wrong hands Mark could be led astray and I feel I've got to watch him.

Rob: It frightens Gaz 'cause Mark always comes out with me!

Gary: It frightens the flaming life out of me that does!

Jason: He does have a potential to stray but he's a good person.

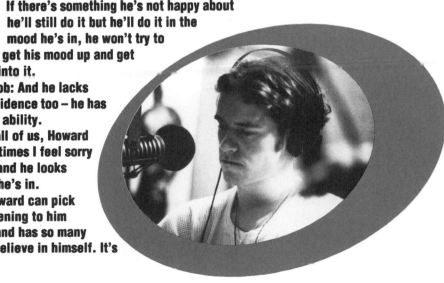

 THE **OTHERS** **ON** **HOWARD**

Gary: You know how Jason says he listens to me, well I listen to Howard more than he realizes. It's always worth asking Howard what he thinks, he's got a very level-headed way about him.

Jason: Very practical thinker. . .

Rob: Very laid back too.

Jason: Sometimes you kind of think, Howard's so basic about things and he's always right. His humour is very basic too. He'll pick on basic things and it's incredibly funny.

Gary: If he can make life easy he will. He doesn't like problems.

Mark: Howard just strolls around and takes every issue and every situation as it comes. I don't think he looks into the future too much. If there's something he's not happy about he'll still do it but he'll do it in the mood he's in, he won't try to get his mood up and get into it.

Rob: And he lacks confidence too – he has so much ability.

Gary: Out of all of us, Howard is the most down to earth and sometimes I feel sorry for him when I see him on the road and he looks quite unhappy to be in the position he's in.

Jason: When Gary writes a tune, Howard can pick any harmony out of it and I love listening to him sing, it's so nice. He's so talented and has so many qualities and he knows he doesn't believe in himself. It's a waste.

COULD YOU BE TAKE THAT'S PERSONAL ASSISTANT?

Imagine it: Take That are so busy that they decide they need a P.A. to be with them night and day. You get the job! But have you got what it takes? Do this quiz and find out. . .

1. Robbie is in the middle of a photo shoot when he suddenly remembers it's his sister's birthday. 'Quick!' he says just as he disappears into makeup, 'send her a bunch of flowers and I'll pay you back later.' When you get to the florist you realize he didn't actually mention his sister's name. It's too late to go back so who do you address the flowers to?

a) Jenny.   **b) Annie.**   **c) Sally.**

2. Jason is starving hungry and asks if you wouldn't mind popping out for a takeaway while he stays in and works out an urgent dance routine. You say you'll be glad to. But which takeaway do you think he'll prefer?

a) Mexican – he adores tortillas.

b) Chinese – he's keen to brush up on his chop stick action.

c) Indian – he's addicted to curry.

3. Take That's manager, Nigel, has bought the lads a tea time snack while they are working in the studio. Just as he's about to hand them round, he gets a phone call. 'Give these to the lads, please,' he says, and hands you three ham sandwiches and two cheese and salad ones. Which Take Thats do you give the cheese and salad to?

a) Gary and Mark – they both love pigs and would never eat ham.

b) Robbie and Howard – they're both allergic to ham.

c) Jason and Mark – they're both vegetarian.

4. Rob is fed up. His football team have lost a match against the rival team. 'I know,' says Jason, 'let's cheer him up by buying him a new footie scarf. Here's a tenner.' When you get to the sports shop which team scarf do you ask for?

a) Accrington Stanley.

b) Port Vale.

c) Stoke City.

5. It's the end of a particularly gruelling tour. You've dropped all the lads off at their houses and you're just checking the tour bus to make sure no one's left anything behind. You look under the seats and find a small silver earring. Who's house do you drive back to in order to return it?

a) Howard's.

b) Gary's.

c) Mark's.

6. Backstage at a concert, there's a phone call. 'It's someone called Jennifer for one of the group,' says the crotchety old commissionaire. 'I didn't catch who she wanted to talk to.' Who do you go and fetch?

a) Mark – it's his mum's sister, Auntie Jenny, who always phones him before a gig to wish him luck.

b) Robbie – Jenny is one of his student mates.

c) Jason – it's his mum.

7. *Gary is worried about Oliver. He's had a cold and is pretty poorly. 'Could you phone my mum and check he's OK?' he asks you. You say you'll be glad to. But who will you be asking about?*

a) His older brother, Ian 'Oliver' Barlow, so named after tubby comedian Oliver Hardy.

b) His beloved doggie.

c) His favourite great uncle, Oliver Barlow.

8. *A journalist is interviewing Mark but the interview has run over time. You usher Mark out of the room and into a waiting car to whisk him off to do a performance on Top Of The Pops. You go back inside to say goodbye to the journalist who says, 'I got everything except the name of the lizard. You couldn't fill me in could you?' What do you say?*

a) I can't tell you, Mark's very secretive about his pets.

b) It's called Nirvana after the famous Seattle group.

c) He hasn't got a lizard any more, his mum made him give it away.

9. *Only Fools And Horses is on TV. 'Go and get whatsisface,' says Howard. 'He'll want to see this.' Who do you fetch?*

a) Jason – because it's his favourite TV show.

b) Nigel, their manager, because he also manages Nicholas Lyndhurst.

c) Gus, their tour manager, because David Jason is his cousin.

10. The group have to be at a local Manchester restaurant at lunchtime to have a meeting with their A&R man, Nick. They all decide to drive to the location in their cars. All except for one, that is. Who do you have to order a cab for?

a) Robbie – he's the only That not to have passed his driving test.

b) Howard – his car recently failed its MOT.

c) Jason – he got a three year driving ban after he was caught speeding last year.

11. You are handing out the That's wage packets. For a joke, their manager has addressed them to two members of the group using their nicknames. On the two envelopes in question it says The B Lander on one and The T Lander on the other. Who do you give them to?

a) Mark and Howard – they're called The Bully Lander and The Terror Lander because they're always landing playful punches on one another.

b) Rob and Gary – they're called The Barf Lander and the Timid Lander because they're both scared of crashing in an aeroplane.

c) Gary and Jason – they're called the B Lander and The T Lander after Gaz watched the Highlander once and thought it was a great 'joke'.

12. Mark is going through his old photo album picking out some baby pictures for a magazine article. He comes across one of him sitting in the front room when he was just a toddler. 'Oh, look, there's Snowy. I remember him, he was so lovely,' he sighs, gazing at the shot. Who does he mean?

a) His great uncle Snowy Owen, so called because his hair went white when he was just 18.

b) Snowy, the family pet rabbit.

c) Snowy, the cat he grew up with.

THE PERSONAL BITS

HOWARD

THE SCENE:
We're sitting in Nigel's garden on a cloudy day. Howard's wearing a pair of jeans and a plain white shirt which he's dead proud of because he just ironed it himself! And – spook! – he's got a few days off so he's decided to grow a goatee and moustache à la Jason. Rob is playing with Nigel's three dogs a few yards away and later on, one of them decides she is in love with Howard and wants to slobber all over him every five minutes. Howard doesn't sound very convincing when he tells the dog to buzz off because he's such a softy. And the dog knows it!

WHAT'S YOUR FULL NAME? *Howard Paul Donald.*

WHAT COLOUR EYES DO YOU HAVE? *Green.*

HOW MUCH DO YOU WEIGH? *About 12 stone 2lbs.*

WHERE DO YOU LIVE? *In Manchester with my family.*

WHAT'S YOUR INSIDE LEG MEASUREMENT? *I think it's about 33" but I get my trousers about two inches longer.*

HOW TALL ARE YOU? *Six foot.*

WHAT'S WITH THE HAIR, THEN? *I think I'm into sticking it back on the top of my head at the moment and that's what I'll keep doing 'til I get bored of it. I wanna keep on growing it but once it starts looking a mess I'll get it cut. You don't think it looks like a mess now, do you?*

WHAT'S YOUR SHOE SIZE? *Nine.*

DO YOU WEAR BOXER SHORTS OR BRIEFS? *Briefs. Boxer shorts are too uncomfortable. You can get the long-legged ones but I prefer the more skimpy ones. I wear designer ones but only because they're more comfortable.*

DO YOU DARN YOUR OWN SOCKS? *Do I what? No. Any socks I get holes in I throw away.*

WHAT DO YOU SPEND YOUR MONEY ON? *Well, I spend it on equipment for my recording studio which I'm building up at the moment. It's half there. I've only been doing it for two years at the most. It's half there. I want a recording studio that I can make good demos in. I also spend my money on petrol, giving my mum my keep, cinema sometimes... that's basically it. I don't really spend lots of money when I go abroad. I bought a few things in New York, there was some quite good stuff there but I can't be doing with the money.*

WHAT'S YOUR WORST HOUSEHOLD CHORE? *Ironing. I hate it. Everything takes so long. Usually when I'm at home my mum irons my clothes but they went away recently and I had two weeks to myself in the house and I had to iron my own shirts. I didn't make too bad a job of it, actually. I did all the washing and the cooking myself. I'm willing to learn all about housework because I'm gonna have to do it when I move into a house by myself.*

WHO'S YOUR FAVOURITE RELATIVE? *My nephew Jamie because he's small and cute and gorgeous and he's only three and I wish he was my son instead.* (At this point, the dog makes a bee-line for Howard and shakes gunge and saliva over everyone.) *No, go away!*

WHO DO YOU LOVE? *All my family really. Because of the people they are. I think I'm lucky to have landed the mum I've got. She raised four children when my dad left her. She'd have to be special to be able to do that and cope with it.*

WHAT'S YOUR MOST VIVID CHILDHOOD MEMORY? *I don't think there's one particular memory as such but I remember we used to go on holiday every year without fail to Wales with my dad and if we went somewhere else I used to be dead upset about it! Go away!* (The dog again.)

WHAT'S YOUR IDEA OF PURE BLISS? *Having my own home. With everything in it. All my gear around me. Also - no! go away! Go away! go on! (Dog again!) - I know that if I could buy my own home then I would have achieved something through doing this to be able to afford it. Oh this dog - go away!*

WHO'S YOUR BEST FRIEND? *Joff. Jonathan Crabtree. I've got a few good friends but Joff is the one whose house I go to if I go anywhere and he's the one I go out with. He understands it now, it would be quite hard for me to make friends with someone new who doesn't understand my job. Whereas he knows and understands everything to it really.*

IF YOU HAD ONE WISH WHAT WOULD IT BE? *That I could fly. Just like Superman. Imagine the freedom. I'd love that more than anything.*

WHAT WOULD YOU DO TO MAKE THE WORLD A BETTER PLACE? *Clear up all the civil wars because civil wars are like a gateway to starvation.*

IS BEING A POP STAR WORTH THE TROUBLE? *Yeah. I think it is because I compare my old job that I was doing beforehand and all the fun I wasn't having to what I'm doing now and all the fun I am having now.*

WHAT ARE YOU FANATICAL ABOUT? *I'm an Indian food fanatic and I'm a boxing fanatic as well. I really like watching boxing. I'd like to do it. I'd like to do kick boxing actually. I used to do it. I did it for about two years. I was quite good at it actually. I stopped because it was in Rochdale and it was about three quarters of an hour bus ride from where I used to work and my brother used to give me a lift sometimes and he stopped going so I had to stop going too.*

DO YOU EVER WISH YOU DID ANOTHER JOB? *There's a lot of the time when I wish I never did anything - not be on the dole but just do nothing and be lazy. I'd have loved to have been a pilot, maybe an RAF pilot, but I know that you need more than two brain cells for that.*

IF YOU COULD CHANGE ONE THING ABOUT YOURSELF WHAT WOULD IT BE? *More organized. I think that's why it would be good for me to get my own home. It'll be a shock to the system as well.*

IF YOU COULD PICK A FIRST NAME FOR YOURSELF WHAT WOULD IT BE? *I like Owen as a first name. Or Brent.*

WHAT'S THE MOST EMBARRASSING ITEM OF CLOTHING YOU HAD TO WEAR AS A KID? *I had a pair of brown corduroy pants that were flared at the bottom, they had a pocket on the leg at the front with a big flower on them. I just wore what my mum got. I wasn't into fashion. They looked terrible though. Go away! (Guess who?)*

WHAT'S YOUR NICKNAME? *Mine's either Dinky Donald or Dougie. Why? I don't know. Barlow made it up and it doesn't make any sense.*

IF YOU COULD BE IN ANY GROUP FROM ANOTHER ERA WHICH WOULD IT BE? *I think The Beatles because they were normal and down to earth. I'd like to have been Paul McCartney.*

WHAT'S YOUR CHAT-UP LINE? *I haven't got a chat-up line. I think I have to get drunk first to approach a girl. But if I like her I'll approach her and I think I'd just ask for her phone number.*

DO YOU THINK IT'S ALL RIGHT FOR GIRLS TO ASK BLOKES OUT? *Yeah.* (Rob interrupts: *Did you ask girls out at school?* Howard: *No, it was an all-boys school!* Rob: *Oh. Didn't any of your mates dress up in frocks as a top turn?* Howard and Rob spend the next five minutes chuckling at this 'joke'.) *Yeah I think girls should be more forward.*

WHAT'S YOUR FAVOURITE SANDWICH FILLING? *Tuna fish and onion with brown sauce on white bread, gorgeous. I also like cheese and onion toasted sandwiches with Branston pickle.*

WHAT DO YOU BELIEVE IN? *I believe in ghosts. I'd really like to see one. I don't think it would frighten me.*

WHAT REALLY GETS ON YOUR NERVES? *I don't like bad table manners - especially people who eat with their mouths open and you can see all their food.*

DO YOU PRAY? *I don't pray at all.*

WOULD YOU DO IT ALL AGAIN? *No, I wouldn't, you know. Because I'm comfortable now. I couldn't do it all again.*

HAVE YOU EVER BEEN IN A SCARY SITUATION WITH A FAN? *Yeah, quite recently actually. I was in my house and I heard these two fans that had been waiting around all day - not like the really nice ones who wait around, you give them an autograph and say hi and then they leave you in peace - these two just weren't going to go away and I heard them saying, "When he gets out here we're gonna punch his lights out." I mean, what's the point of that?*

WHAT DO YOU HATE THAT JOURNALISTS SAY ABOUT YOU? *I hate it when a journalist prints lies about you. Or if they think they've found out something about you and they think they've got you cornered. I hate it when they try to put you on the spot, too.*

HOW DO YOU SEE YOURSELF WHEN YOU'RE 70? *I know this is not possible but I'd really like to be as fit as I am now even when I'm 70. To still be working out and being active. I was in a cafe the other day and I saw this old bloke with a cup of tea and his hands were shaking and I knew that I would end up like that one day, bound to, you can't stop it happening. But I wish it wouldn't.*

ThE PERSonal BiTs

ROBBIE

THE SCENE:

Rob's in one of those moods. He's cracking a joke a minute and to distract him even further, he's got a mosquito bite at the top of his leg which he keeps scratching and getting everyone else to look at. We're in Nigel's garden. One of his dogs, Wooly, keeps coming up for a kiss. "Kiss me Wooly, you love me best," Rob keeps saying. He's wearing a pair of immense trainers with no laces, some swanky pale blue and dark blue stripy shorts, and a white vest through which he keeps flexing his chest.

WHAT'S YOUR FULL NAME? *Robert Peter Williams.*

WHAT COLOUR ARE YOUR EYES? *Green, like Howard's.*

HOW TALL ARE YOU? *6' 1".*

WHAT'S WITH THE HAIR? *Well, it's brown, just like Howard's. In fact we look like brothers really. I don't know what's happening to my hair. I know that's awful, innit? Who knows? I get shouted at and told to cut it so I'll probably cut it all off.*

HOW MUCH DO YOU WEIGH? *I never disclose my weight.*

WHAT'S YOUR INSIDE LEG MEASUREMENT? *33", like Howard – ooh, look at the bite on my leg. It's really itchy* (proceeds to scratch bite furiously).

WHERE DO YOU LIVE? *Stoke-on-Trent with my family.*

WHAT SIZE SHOES DO YOU TAKE? *10.*

DO YOU WEAR BOXER SHORTS OR BRIEFS? *I wear briefs. I used to wear boxers but now I like the short-cut briefs. I wear designer ones – Calvins because they're comfortable and comfort comes from within – within your pants!*

DO YOU DARN YOUR OWN SOCKS? *No. I throw them away because I'm bound to get holes in them in about ten seconds and then when I buy new ones I leave them in hotel rooms anyway. So the sock situation is a disaster.*

WHAT DO YOU SPEND YOUR MONEY ON? *I was going to say going down the pub and having a laugh as a bit of a joke to make you titter and everything and then I realized that that is what I spend my money on. And clothes and roller blades and CDs.*

WHAT'S YOUR WORST HOUSEHOLD CHORE? *Washing the dishes and wiping them. Do I have to do any housework? Well, no.*

DO YOU ACTUALLY DO ANYTHING FOR YOURSELF AT HOME? *No. I'm actually finding it quite embarrassing because I hang about with a few student friends of mine and they were telling me about a friend of theirs whose limit of cooking is cheese on toast and I looked them and said, "You are kidding!" And then I thought, well what can I make? Not even that.*

WHO'S YOUR FAVOURITE RELATIVE? *It's difficult to say but I'm gonna say my cousin Tony. He's about 33, 34.*

WHAT'S YOUR MOST VIVID CHILDHOOD MEMORY? *I used to enjoy going on caravan sites with my dad. He was like a compere and entertainments manager and everything. I used to love going on the sites with him but unfortunately I can't do that any more.*

WHO DO YOU LOVE? *I love my mum and my sister, Sally. I love them both and I'm always telling them I love them.*

WHAT'S YOUR IDEA OF PURE BLISS? *It's got to be a beach. And sun. Beach, sun and a Cuba Libra in your hand. If Stoke-on-Trent was by a beach and it was hot, that would be pure bliss. Stoke's bliss.*

WHO'S YOUR BEST FRIEND? *I've got a few but I suppose it's got to be my sister Sally or my mum. Why Sally? She's my mate, you know, we knock about and that. We're like best mates. She comes down the pub with me and we just have a laugh together.*

IF YOU HAD ONE WISH WHAT WOULD IT BE? *The thing that I'd wish for is world peace, but you know what I mean, everyone says that, so I'm going to say that I hope Vale go into Europe. But the obvious one is world peace.*

WHAT WOULD YOU DO TO MAKE THE WORLD A BETTER PLACE? *I'd get rid of all the selfish wealthy people.*

IS BEING A POP STAR WORTH THE TROUBLE? *There's no trouble really. Not really when you think about it. I compare it to being at school. I wish I'd had about three or four years of doing a proper job so that I could really appreciate what I'm doing because I do appreciate now when I'm able to go out and buy clothes that I like or go up to the golf course and have a round of golf but I still find it weird that I'm not at school during the days. Like I'll be at home and by about 11.00am I'm doing nothing. I think I should be at school.*

WHAT ARE YOU FANATICAL ABOUT? *What do you think I'm fanatical about? PVFC. Port Vale FC! I've got nothing against Stoke City. I want that to be known. But I support PVFC. I've supported them ever since I could acknowledge football greatness. I've met the players. When I was sixteen I used to go to the matches and hang around outside the players' exit for them to come out and they'd sign autographs.*

DO YOU EVER WISH YOU DID ANOTHER JOB? *No, this is my job, man. This is what I do. I mean, I never knew that I'd be this famous, but I knew I was going to do something in entertainment. I'd probably be a Blue Coat by now you know, on one of my dad's camps probably.*

IF YOU COULD CHANGE ONE THING ABOUT YOURSELF WHAT WOULD IT BE? *I'm so forgetful. I forget at least three very important things a week. Like I lost my wallet with all my credit cards and thirty quid that I won and I've lost a jacket - untold jackets and trousers.*

IF YOU COULD PICK A FIRST NAME FOR YOURSELF WHAT WOULD IT BE? *Jack, after my grandad. Jack Farrell. Big Jack.*

WHAT'S THE MOST EMBARRASSING ITEM OF CLOTHING YOU HAD TO WEAR AS A KID? *I can remember seeing a picture of me going to our cousin Jane's wedding. I was put into these tartan trousers with flares at the bottom and a shirt made out of that terrible material - what's it called? It squeaks when you rub it? Viscose, yeah - it had a great big rocket ship on the chest and I had a massive big tie and a massive collar.*

WHAT'S YOUR NICKNAME? *Scabble. I don't know why. This lot call it me. And Scab. And Bob. I like Bob. Bob's good. Barlow makes 'em up and they don't make any sense at all.*

IF YOU WERE A JOURNALIST WHICH QUESTION WOULD YOU ASK YOURSELF? *I'd like to be asked, "What do you think about the comparisons between you and New Kids On The Block?" because, you know, I've never been asked that one before. It's never cropped up. I've never been asked that. I wouldn't know what to say because I'd be completely baffled and I've never even seen the New Kids On The Block. I don't know who they are. Seriously, I thought we'd got all that behind us but when we went to America that's all we got asked all over again. It drove us mad.*

IF YOU COULD BE IN ANY GROUP FROM ANOTHER ERA WHICH WOULD IT BE? *The Beatles. I'd like to be Paul because he's just a top laugh. He was dead funny. And so was John. And so were Ringo and George really.*

WHAT'S YOUR CHAT-UP LINE? *I haven't got one. It's normally goodnight. Goodnight. Goodnight love. 'Cause like, there was this girl at a discotheque the other night and I was looking at her across the floor and she was looking at me all night. So I went over to her at the end and said, goodnight and walked off. No, it wasn't very nice but it was a top laugh.*

IS IT ALL RIGHT FOR GIRLS TO ASK BLOKES OUT? *God yes. I know when I was at school I wished girls would have asked me out because I was so shy at asking girls out. It's all supposed to be equal. I think more so now in the 90s. Everyone has rights, women's rights, men's rights, every right, right of way.*

WHAT'S YOUR FAVOURITE SANDWICH FILLING? *Now it was ham and Branston pickle. I used to eat that all the time. Now I like cheese and onion and Branston pickle. I think I prefer that.*

WHAT DO YOU BELIEVE IN? *I believe in good and evil. I believe that we all have a good spirit and a bad spirit and I believe that everyone is capable of being evil because it's in us all the time but you have to control it.*

WHAT REALLY GETS ON YOUR NERVES? *I'll tell you what gets on my nerves: When you pull your nail off and a bit of skin comes off with it and it's all bloody.*

DO YOU PRAY? *Not very often. I'm not very religious at all. I'm a Catholic, believe it or not after that answer, but I'm what's known as a not very good Catholic. I don't think I'll be getting any commendations from the Pope this year. I'm not a practising one.*

HAVE YOU EVER BEEN IN A SCARY SITUATION WITH A FAN? *Yeah, once I was in my house and these fans kept knocking on the door. I didn't open it but they knew I was in there. They kept looking through the letter box. Then they started to chip away at the windowledge, you know the putty round the window, and the window caved in. The next thing I knew they got a chainsaw and started to saw round the foundations of the house and the whole thing collapsed. That's a lie of course. No, I can look after myself most of the time.*

WHAT DO YOU HATE THAT JOURNALISTS SAY ABOUT YOU? *That we're a pop group and nothing else. Now I don't mind being in a pop group – no, I have no worries about being The Kings Of Girlie Bloke Pop. That's great, but some people are so snobbish about it, papers like the NME who think we're some joke and that we're not good enough because we're not Suede or some Indie band.*

HOW DO YOU SEE YOURSELF WHEN YOU'RE 70? *I'd like to be clubbing.*

NOSEY NOSEY NOSEY NOSEY NOSEY

THE RULES:
The boys each get the key word or question and say the first thing that comes into their head.

JASON: I like to exercise in the morning and the evening — not every morning or evening. I like to do sit ups, press ups, I don't use weights, I just like using my own body weight. And I dance.
ROB: Yeah, I'm a big lad. I like to swim and rollerblade but I don't get as much exercise as I'd like to and I'll probably be a fat waster by the time I'm 26.
JASON: He's a big lad isn't he? He's naturally big and muscly.
MARK: I sometimes go through phases where I say right I'm gonna exercise every day and then I do it for a couple of weeks and then just don't bother. When I do exercise I do sit ups and press ups, leg raises. And I like swimming, I find it the nicest form of exercise.
HOWARD: (The rest of the group call him The Body) Oh I hate that! Please don't call me that. Like J, I like to use my own body weight and I don't like to use weights. I do sit ups, press ups, leg raises. I wish I could do more stamina exercises like running but I find running so boring. I like going swimming. The reason I do exercises during interviews or photo shoots is because I'm too tired to do them in the evening when I get home and I don't want to do my exercises just before I eat because I find I'm not hungry and I don't like to do it after I've eaten 'cause I feel like I'll be sick.
GARY: Exercise?

SOUND AND VISION

MARK: In my room I've got a telly, a hi-fi which only cost £200 – I got it with my first wages from the bank, it's probably worth a tenner now – a Walkman, electric razor, keyboard.

ROB: I've got a stereo that cost a hundred pounds and the sound keeps going. I think it's an Amstrad. I'd like a posh one but they're too expensive. I had a Discman and I was listening to it while I was on a sun bed and the ultraviolet rays broke the laser so it's knackered. And I've got a telly in my room.

GARY: I've got a lot of electrical stuff in my studio. But I've got two stereos, a Hitachi and a Phillips, the Phillips is the best. I'd like a Discman. I'd like a TV in my bedroom but I haven't got one and I've got a real old TV that my old lady gave me. I haven't got flash tellies or anything. I would like a Bang and Olufsen set-up but it would have to be if I buy another house. I've got a microwave, though.

JASON: I've got a Walkman, a dictaphone and a camera. I've got no music equipment because I'm living in my brother's flat and so I use his. When I get my own place I'll sort it out. I don't own a TV or video for the same reasons.

HOWARD: I've got a Walkman, a telly in my room, a hi-fi and I've also got a keyboard and all the other stuff for the studio I'm building up.

JEWELLERY

JASON: One necklace — my bone beads and my ring — a black onyx and silver hand carved one-off I got in Manchester.
GARY: This gold chain, Nige bought it for my 21st birthday. It's the only chain I ever wear really.
ROB: My Take That jewellery and, in fact, all the jewellery in the Top Man range!
MARK: I like silver jewellery.
HOWARD: There's a few chains I wear. I used to wear my Take That chain but I took it off because I'm not really into gold. I've just bought a nice ring from Germany too.

HOWARD: Pickled onion piglets or Seabrook's salt 'n' vinegar crinkle cut crisps.
MARK: Nice 'n' spicy what're they called? The brown ones — Nick Nacks.
JASON: I don't like crisps (but a few days later he devours three packets of cheese snacks like they're going out of fashion).
GARY: Oh I do. . . I like cheese and onion Ringos and I can't find them anywhere.
ROB: I like Skips prawn cocktail thingies by KP. I also like the chip thingies — no, not chipsticks. . .
JASON: He means the little fish and chips you get.
MARK: Yeah, fish and chips. You get a little fish and a little chip. . .
ROB: No, I don't mean them! Oh forget it!

JASON: My beads.

GARY: I also think of my chain from Nige as being a bit of a lucky charm, when Nigel bought it we had a hit with It Only Takes A Minute.

ROB: My chest. Never be without my chest.

MARK: I picked up a pouch in Acapulco from this hippy girl we met there called Christine. It's got three stones in it and Rob's got one too.

HOWARD: I think my underwear's a bit of a lucky charm. Any underwear that I wear because it's nice underwear and I feel quite good in it.

LUCKY CHARMS

VIBES

JASON: The colour blue. I'm comfortable in blue clothing, I'm comfortable in blue surroundings.

GARY: Writing a good song. You don't know it's good until everyone's heard it but then you feel great.

ROB: I can remember once when the Vale won that I got a good vibe. I get good vibes all the time.

MARK: Music.

ROB: Yeah funky music, music's good.

HOWARD: Like Gary it gives me a good vibe when I write a good song because I know I'm learning all the time.

TV SHOW/FILM

JASON: Only Fools And Horses or Mr Bean and film would be The Krays or Awakenings.

ROB: The Lost Boys I think is my favourite film and I'd like to say The Fresh Prince Of Bel Air but I've never watched it! EastEnders I'm really intrigued by.

GARY: I like Saturday Zoo with Jonathan Ross on a Saturday night.

ROB: It hasn't been on for about two years.

GARY: No, but it's good when it's on. And my film is Awakenings, definitely.

MARK: I like The Outsiders as a film and The Simpsons on the telly.

HOWARD: Favourite programmes are The Word, Big Breakfast or Mr Bean and film. . . Born On The Fourth Of July or The Commitments.

TOOTHPASTE

EVERYONE: COLGATE BLUE MINTY GEL.
MARK: I ALSO LIKE SIGNAL AND AQUAFRESH.

JASON: Pink Floyd's Obscured By Clouds, one of the early ones.

ROB: My favourite at the moment is The Digable Planets.

GARY: I suppose my favourite album to listen through the whole thing is Seal's album. Called Seal.

MARK: The album I like most is the newest Sade album.

HOWARD: Mine's Dark Side Of The Moon by Pink Floyd or The Best Of The Police or Ten Summoner's Tales by Sting.

word or phrase

ROB: Just recently I've been using this word 'ode'. Hello ode.
MARK: I say 'take care'.
HOWARD: You say 'to be honest' too. I use 'you know' a lot.
JASON: 'Y'alright?'
GARY: 'It's funny really'.

TOYS

HOWARD: I wrecked all my toys or sold them for money when I was a kid!
MARK: I passed all my toys on to my younger brother and sister and other relatives.
ROB: A broken guitar from when I was a kid.
JASON: I haven't got any toys but I did find an old sewing machine in the loft. I'm hanging on to it because it's probably an antique.
GARY: I've got my first teddy bear. What's it called? I dunno. Teddy I s'pose. A little white one, it's quite nice, quite cute.

ICE CREAM

JASON: I don't like ice cream.
ROB: I love all sorts apart from chocolate.
MARK: I'm not a lover of chocolate either, the rest I can handle. And coffee I hate.
GARY: All of it. Just feed it to me with a funnel.
HOWARD: I used to like the Funny Feet Ice creams on sticks.
GARY (going into a bit of a reverie): Oh yeah... with the chocolate toe.... oh yeah... and have you ever had a Rock Around The Choc? With all them bobbles on the outside. Oh...
HOWARD: Mr Men I always used to have, the green ones.
ROB: Fab, Fab are coming back big time, good call.

SWEETS

HOWARD: I like Trebor sherbet fountains.
MARK: Double Deckers.
JASON: Licorice or Midget Gems.
GARY: All my favourite sweets I can't eat any more because I've given up chocolate. I used to like Dairy Milk and Drifters.
ROB: I like Drifters.

BOOK

JASON: The Lion The Witch And The Wardrobe. The whole set of Narnia books - I haven't read them all but I want to.
ROB: The Lord Of The Rings and I've read the whole trilogy. What's that book where he goes in to save the negro and he is the lawyer? Who goes in? The fella, the fella goes in and supports negroes, you know? (The rest of the group help him out with various suggestions as to what he might be rambling on about but to no avail. He probably means To Kill A Mocking Bird by Harper Lee, however.) Oh, just say A Crime Of Passion, The Krays.
GARY: I like either The Firm or The Fourth Protocol by Frederick Forsyth. Have you read it? It's really good.
MARK: No One Gets Out Of Here Alive. I can't remember who it's by but it's about Jim Morrison (bloke from ancient 60s group The Doors).
HOWARD: I've never actually read a full book. I remember reading half way through a Vietnam book which was very interesting but I never finished it.

SHOES

JASON: My cowboy boots that I bought in New York recently for $90.
GARY: My Next boots. £24.
ROB: I like anything from Red Or Dead. And Adidas trainers.
MARK: I just like boots in general but when it gets hot I like to wear Converse boots.
HOWARD: These German army boots, £20 from an Army And Navy store - the strongest boots I've ever had. I've had 'em for years.

TOILETRIES YOU COULDN'T DO WITHOUT

EVERYONE: Toothpaste.. Actually no, it's a toothbrush. You can always borrow toothpaste from another person but I don't like
HOWARD: Actually no, it's a toothbrush. You can always borrow toothpaste from another person but I don't like borrowing a toothbrush.
GARY: Good call Dougie!

THREE WORDS TO DESCRIBE YOURSELF

JASON: Honest, sensitive, committed.
ROB: Cheeky, silly and shy.
GARY: Committed, ambitious, down to earth.
MARK: Caring, worrier and small.
HOWARD: Nice, disorganized and creative.

Hello again

Well, there you go. I hope you enjoyed your read (I used to enjoy reading the 'Beano' annual myself)

We've been out of the country for a big part of this year yet we've still received the best support from our British fans. This is a nice time for me to say — Thankyou...

We hope we can do many more annuals for many more years but if not there's always the 'Beano'

Bye bye, Love Jason
x

Out of all the annuals I've ever read, this is definitely one of them. Thankyou for staying awake and thankyou for once again supporting Take That. Love as always

Gaz
xxx

CHEERS! (4 EVERYTHING!)
All THE BEST
BOB